Those were the days ... ™

British Police Cars

Nick Walker

VELOCE PUBLISHING
THE PUBLISHER OF FINE AUTOMOTIVE BOOKS

Also from Veloce Publishing –

Colour Family Album Series
Alfa Romeo by Andrea & David Sparrow
Bubblecars & Microcars by Andrea & David Sparrow
Bubblecars & Microcars, More by Andrea & David Sparrow
Citroen 2CV by Andrea & David Sparrow
Citroen DS by Andrea & David Sparrow
Fiat & Abarth 500 & 600 by Andrea & David Sparrow
Lambretta by Andrea & David Sparrow
Motor Scooters by Andrea & David Sparrow
Porsche by Andrea & David Sparrow
Triumph Sportscars by Andrea & David Sparrow
Vespa by Andrea & David Sparrow
VW Beetle by Andrea & David Sparrow
VW Beetle/Bug, Custom by Andrea & David Sparrow
VW Bus, Camper, Van & Pick-up by Andrea & David Sparrow

SpeedPro Series
4-Cylinder Engine Short Block for High Performance, How to Blueprint & Build a by Des Hammill
Alfa Romeo Twin Cam Engines, How to Power Tune by Jim Kartalamakis
BMC/BL/Rover 998cc A-Series Engines, How to Power Tune by Des Hammill
BMC/BL/Rover 1275cc A-Series Engines, How to Power Tune by Des Hammill
Camshafts for Maximum Power, How to Choose & Time by Des Hammill
Cylinder Heads, How to Build, Modify & Power Tune (2nd edition) by Peter Burgess
Distributor-type Ignition Systems, How to Build & Power Tune by Des Hammill
Ford SOHC 'Pinto' & Sierra Cosworth DOHC Engines, How to Power Tune (2nd Edition) by Des Hammill
Harley-Davidson 1340 Evolution Engines, How to Build & Power Tune by Des Hammill
Jaguar XK Engines, How to Power Tune by Des Hammill
MGB 4-Cylinder Engines, How to Power Tune by Peter Burgess
MGB, MGC, MGB V8, How to Improve by Roger Williams
MGB V8 Power, How to Give your (Updated & Revised Edition) by Roger Williams
MG Midget & Austin-Healey Sprite for Road & Track, How to Power Tune by Daniel Stapleton
Mini Engines, How to Power Tune on a Small Budget by Des Hanmmill
Road Car, How to Plan & Build a Fast by Daniel Stapleton
Sportscar/Kitcar Suspension and Brakes, How to Build and Modify by Des Hammill
SU Carburettors for High Performance, How to Build and Modify (Revised Edition) by Des Hammill
Weber DCOE & Dellorto DHLA Carburetors, How to Build & Power Tune (2nd edition) by Des Hammill
VW Beetle, How to Modify Suspension, Brakes & Chassis for High Performance by James Hale
V8 Engine Short Block for High Performance, How to Blueprint & Build by Des Hammill

Enthusiast's Restoration Manual Series
How to Restore Triumph TR3 & 3A by Roger Williams
How to Restore Triumph TR4 & 4A by Roger Williams
How to Restore Triumph TR5, 250 & 6 by Roger Williams

General
Alfa Romeo Berlinas (Saloons/Sedans) by John Tipler
Alfa Romeo Giulia Coupe GT & GTA by John Tipler
Automotive Mascots: A Collectors Guide to British Marque, Corporate & Accessory Mascots
  by David Kay & Lynda Springate
Bentley Continental Corniche & Azure 1951-1998 by Martin Bennett
BMW Z-Cars by James Taylor
British Cars, The Complete Catalogue of 1895-1975 by Culshaw & Horrobin

British Police Cars by Nick Walker
British Trailer Caravans & their Manufacturers 1919-1959 by Andrew Jenkinson
British Trailer Caravans & their Manufacturers from 1960 by Andrew Jenkinson
Bugatti Type 40 by Barrie Price & Jean Louis Arbey
Bugatti 46/50, Updated & Revised Edition by Barrie Price
Bugatti 57, The Last French Bugatti, 2nd Edition by Barrie Price & Jean Louis Arbey
Chrysler 300 - America's Most Powerful Car by Robert Ackerson
Cobra - The Real Thing! by Trevor Legate
Cortina - Ford's Best Seller by Graham Robson
Daimler SP250 'Dart' by Brian Long
Datsun/Nissan 280ZX & 300ZX by Brian Long
Datsun Z - From Fairlady to 280Z by Brian Long
Dune Buggy Handbook, The by James Hale
Fiat & Abarth 124 Spider & Coupe by John Tipler
Fiat & Abarth 500 & 600 (revised edition) by Malcolm Bobbitt
Ford F100/F150 Pick-up by Robert Ackerson
Ford Model Y - Henry's Car for Europe by Sam Roberts
Jaguar XJ-S by Brian Long
Jim Redman - Six Times World Motorcycle Champion by Jim Redman
Land-Rover, Half-ton Military by Mark Cook
Lea-Francis Story, The by Barrie Price
Lexus by Brian Long
Lola - The Illustrated History (1957-1977) by John Starkey
Lola - All Sports Racing Cars & Single-seaters 1978-1997 by John Starkey
Lola T70 - The Racing History & Individual Chassis Record New Edition by John Starkey
Lotus 49, The Story of a Legend by Michael Oliver
Mazda MX5/Miata 1.6 Enthusiast's Workshop Manual by Rod Grainger & Pete Shoemark
Mazda MX5/Miata 1.8 Enthusiast's Workshop Manual by Rod Grainger & Pete Shoemark
Mazda MX5 - Renaissance Sportscar by Brian Long
Mazda RX-7: Mazda's Rotary Engine Sportscar by Brian Long
MGA by John Price Williams
Motor Museums - of the British Isles and Republic of Ireland by David Burke & Tom Price
Mini Cooper - The Real Thing! by John Tipler
Porsche 356 by Brian Long
Porsche 911S, RS & RSR 4th Ed. by John Starkey
Porsche 914 & 914-6 by Brian Long
Porsche 924 by Brian Long
Porsche 944 by Brian Long
Rolls-Royce Silver Shadow & Bentley T-Series Updated & Revised Edition by Malcolm Bobbitt
Rolls-Royce Silver Spirit, Silver Spur and Bentley Mulsanne by Malcolm Bobbitt
Rolls-Royce Silver Wraith, Dawn & Cloud/Bentley MkVI, R & S-Series by Martyn Nutland
Singer Story: Cars, Commercial Vehicles, Bicycles & Motorcycles by Kevin Atkinson
Tales of Triumph Motorcycles by Hughie Hancox
Taxi! The Story of the 'London' Taxicab by Malcolm Bobbitt
Triumph Tiger Cub Bible by Mike Estall
Triumph TR6 by William Kimberley
Turner's Triumphs by Jeff Clew
Velocette Motorcycles - MSS to Thruxton by Rod Burris
Volkswagens of the World by Simon Glen
VW Bus, Camper, Van, Pickup, Wagon (Type 2) by Malcolm Bobbitt
Volkswagen Beetle - The Car of the 20th Century by Richard Copping
Works Minis, The Anatomy of the, by Brian Moylan
Works Rally Mechanic, Tales of the BMC/BL Works Rally Department 1955-1979 by Brian Moylan

First published in 2001. Veloce Publishing Ltd., 33 Trinity Street, Dorchester DT1 1TT, England. Fax 01305 268864. E-mail: info@veloce.co.uk. Web: www.veloce.co.uk/www.velocebooks.com
ISBN 1-903706-01-7/UPC 36847-00201-5

Contents

It seems likely that the first registration in Worcestershire, AB 1, issued in 1903, was used for the Chief Constable's car. Certainly it was so by about 1907, when his car was the Humber shown here. However, this was the second vehicle to use the mark, the first having been a 5hp single-cylinder Wolseley in 1903.

British Police Cars

At a time when most prison vans were horse-drawn, this must have been one of the very earliest motorised versions. It is a De Dion, used by the Bedfordshire County force, and it is shown here with its crew in the prison yard at Bedford in 1913.

Foreword

How strange that we should harbour nostalgic feelings towards police cars! For most of us the last thing we want to see is a white-and-orange shape with flashing blue lights filling our mirrors. Yet through time's rose-tinted spectacles the thought of a black Wolseley with a bell above the front bumper is one of life's charming memories. Were policemen more friendly, less impersonal, in those far-off days? Did the sight of a patrol car rushing through the streets mean protection for "us", and retribution for "them", any more than it does nowadays?

Perhaps it is just one more reflection on the pace at which we live our lives today, compared with the more leisurely atmosphere of years ago? Without motorways there was less need for the police to use super-fast cars. When the nearest policeman was only a few streets away he could come on his bike, or even running, rather than respond to a radio call when he is many miles away. And when there were dozens of small police forces and as many (British) car manufacturers, there was a far greater variety in the types of vehicle they chose to use.

Still, for whatever reason, most of us look back with affection at police motoring as it used to be. For some it is the hilarity which catches the imagination - the sight of two large constables in a tiny Morgan three-wheeler, for example. Others are fascinated by the diaspora of police organisation in former times, when every medium-size town had its own separate police force with its own idea of what constituted the ideal car. Arrol-Johnston, Austin, Bentley, Humber, Perry, Railton, Riley, Standard, Wolseley - all these makes and many more have served the forces of law and order, and how many are still with us today?

The organisation of our police forces is still a sensitive subject. Not for nothing did these numerous county and county borough forces lead their separate existences, resisting until the very last moment the calls for amalgamation. Opposition to any idea of a "national" police force is something which runs deep in the psyche of the British nation, and it largely explains why these tiny, inefficient organisations were allowed to continue. The increased mobility of the criminal and the spread of the motorway network, let alone the need for increased efficiency, are three good reasons why change had to come. Yet we can still feel a pang of regret that we are being policed from some faraway headquarters rather than from our own town hall.

The photographs of those times are historical documents in themselves. So often they capture the spirit of the age, quite apart from the cars or the men and women driving them. Surely our attitude to the police, and theirs to us, was different then? The Shropshire constable standing beside his Hillman in Bridgnorth not only has enough time to stay there while the picture is taken, but will probably stay a little longer in case someone wants to come up and talk to him.

Yet if it is true that the period from, say, the twenties to the fifties was the time when there was least antagonism towards the police, why did it change? Was it just the enormous growth in traffic and traffic-related offences, or was it something more fundamental? Did the swinging sixties, when everyone was encouraged to "do his own thing", create a general resistance to the voice of authority? Does the independence of the modern teenager, both financially and otherwise, lead to an instinctive dislike of anyone who tries to tell him or her what to do? Such are the questions which a study of these pictures can provoke, and which can engender some fascinating speculation.

So it is with a mixture of emotions that we contemplate these photographs from times past. Most

British Police Cars

A make of car which long ago passed into history, but which in its day carried considerable prestige, was the Scottish-built Arrol-Johnston. This particular car was new in 1914, and was the personal transport of the Chief Constable of the Bedfordshire Constabulary.

Another early Worcestershire vehicle was this 1916 Perry, probably only the second vehicle in the County force. Here it is conducting Superintendent Rudnick (and his dog) of Bromsgrove around his division. Note the white-topped caps, which after a long absence have made a comeback in more modern times for traffic crew uniforms.

of our thoughts are serious ones: nostalgia for a more leisurely pace of life, regret at our loss of personal contact with the people who police our streets - even some lingering concern that our freedoms are being slowly eroded. In our minds somewhere, too, is the realisation that a British motor industry which could offer a bewildering variety of makes and models has gone forever.

But surely the lighter side of life can never be far from our thoughts? Just how wet did they get in those open MGs? How many times did they accidentally tear the aerial off the top of that wireless lorry? How proud every traffic policeman looks when he is allowed to be photographed beside the section's latest acquisition. And are all policemen such bad actors when they are asked to stage an "incident" for the camera?

In the end, though, throughout this book it is the cars that are the stars. From the earliest Edwardian Humber, through the Wolseleys and Rileys from before and after World War 2, to the comparatively modern Rovers and Granadas of the seventies, each represented someone's concept of the ideal vehicle for the job. Without exception these machines were asked to perform to the utmost of their abilities for hours and days at a time, through rain, ice and snow. As we see them at work we feel nostalgia, yes, but nostalgia tinged with pride in the job they did and which their successors continue to do today.

British Police Cars

Amongst the earliest vehicles used by the Staffordshire County police was this strange Crossley wireless lorry, pictured in about 1920. It is thought to have been "donated" by the War Office after service with the Royal Flying Corps in the First World War.

Opposite page - In the Metropolitan Police, on the other hand, cars were made available to very senior ranks - normally down to superintendent. This Model T Ford was the personal transport of a Superintendent Parker in the early twenties. Naturally he had a driver rather than driving himself.

In the twenties it was often the individual rather than the police force who owned a car. In the Leicestershire force Superintendent Smith of Melton Mowbray was allowed to use his own 1923 Model T Ford on official business. He and the car are seen here in 1926 at a Cottesmore Hunt meet.

Introduction

When the Metropolitan Police Force was set up in London in 1829, and others followed on soon after in the 1830s, the question of mobility simply did not arise. Policemen walked everywhere - it was as simple as that. When we used to talk of bobbies "pounding the beat", it was no idle phrase; the typical constable of the 19th century would often walk twenty miles a day.

And there was no great pressure to change things, even after the motor car had arrived. Horses were only used by exception, and indeed there were not even any specialist "mounted" sections (in other words, equipped with horses) until about 1920. Amazingly, even the use of bicycles was not permitted until the early 1900s. Probably the first vehicle to be seen in any police force would have been a horse-drawn prison van - the original "Black Maria".

Of course cars did play a part in many police forces from the early days. Among the very first were two 7.5hp Wolseley tourers at the "Met", in 1903. These would have been reserved for the use of the most senior officers - Assistant Commissioners - and only on the rarest of occasions for actually catching criminals. Similar purchases in provincial forces were along the same lines, with Chief Constables making a case to their local Watch Committees for the acquisition of a single car - which was of course for the Chief's use only.

Little by little the motor car with a policeman in it became a more common sight. More accurately, it would usually have two policemen inside, since the tradition of a police constable as chauffeur was established early on. First to justify their need for mobility in this way were superintendents, who understandably could see the advantages of being able to travel round their areas with much greater efficiency than by train or horse-drawn dog-cart. By the early twenties it was probably the norm for superintendents to travel by car.

Other kinds of motorised transport for the police also began to make an appearance around this time. Many forces were responsible for fire and ambulance cover as well, so we see examples of both types of vehicle, but always in police livery. Naturally the "Black Maria" came to be motorised during this period. It was also in the twenties that experiments began involving the installation of wireless sets in police vehicles, although the first pieces of equipment were cumbersome in the extreme.

Even in this post-World War 1 period police forces generally were still trying to establish their place in society. The police strikes in 1918 and 1919 led directly

In 1925, as now, Chief Constables were important people. No matter that their sphere of operations was somewhat smaller then; Chief Constable Burrows of the Reading Constabulary, seen here in his Austin tourer, was important in Reading, and that was what mattered.

British Police Cars

Staffordshire force Albion lorries, which are thought to have been "donated" by the War Office. Here they are seen in 1926, one assumes in preparation for use during the General Strike (note the anti-riot protection for the windscreens and cab sides).

Left - Here's an early example of a well-known make - a Standard of about 1926. Part of the Worcestershire County force's fleet, this Rhyl coupé was based at Bromsgrove and appears to have been issued to the divisional superintendent. No lower rank would have been entitled to a car at this period.

Right - A Lea-Francis 14/40 tourer seems an unlikely choice as a police car, even in 1927. As it happens, this particular vehicle is believed to be the very first car used by the famous Flying Squad of the Metropolitan Police. Their good taste in sporting machinery later became legendary.

By 1927 the Metropolitan Police were making cars available to ranks down to the level of inspector. The normal issue was the 7hp Jowett tourer, as seen here lined up outside Ewins Garage, Banbury. At the same time, though, the standard of car seems to have dropped, since some superintendents also had to accept the same model.

Opposite - Hillman was regarded as something of a prestige make in 1929. These 14hp saloons of the Metropolitan Police fleet, lined up outside the old Scotland Yard building, were reserved for use only by the most exalted levels - the Commissioner and Assistant Commissioners, for example, and even the Home Secretary.

to the establishment of the Police Federation, with which went greatly increased pay but also a termination of the right to strike. No-one at that time could have foreseen the General Strike of 1926, but these changes meant that the police continued working while much of the remaining workforce went on strike. The newspaper images of the time, showing policemen protecting volunteers while they carried out essential work, may or may not have enhanced the reputation of the police with the general public.

It is clear, too, that the superiority of the motor vehicle as a means of transport was not universally accepted. Indeed, at the beginning of the twenties quite a number of forces were still setting up mounted branches, often using ex-soldiers with cavalry training. Their role was not immediately obvious, but it was certainly not confined to crowd control - that came later.

The most common sight at this time would therefore have been either a town policeman walking his beat, or

else his rural counterpart mounted on a bicycle. The number of cars and other motorised transport in a police force was still small, and only superintendents and upwards could rely on having a car available to them. What might those cars have been? We have to rely mainly on speculation at this point, since few contemporary records survive. Those that do, in particular the photographs of the period, suggest that there was little consistency from one force to another.

Inevitably, with the norm being a relatively small force serving a "county borough" (*ie* city or larger town) or a county, the Chief Constable would be under pressure to keep any such purchases within the borough boundary. In practice this would mean a fairly limited choice for his force, since there would only be a small number of main agencies from which to choose. Taken over the country as a whole, however, the effect was to produce an infinite variety of makes and models in use by the police. There would be no obvious reason why a

British Police Cars

Swift, for example, should perform any less well than an Argyll or an Austin. So if the local dealer had a Swift agency, that would be the make which the Chief would probably select.

So the early period of police motoring saw Chief Constables, their assistants, and superintendents all enjoying the benefit of being able to travel by motor car. Lower ranks, however, were less fortunate; the luckier ones went by train, bus or bicycle, the others had to walk. Unless, of course, you were the driver of a prison van or wireless lorry or mobile canteen, in which case you could look forward to going round the countryside in nearly as much luxury as your superintendent.

Separate traffic patrols (known originally as "motor patrols") were not yet seen as necessary. Of course the motorist had been breaking the law since the invention of motoring, but up to now he (they were usually men) could still be caught by time-honoured means - speed-traps, licence inspections and so on. The complexities of the Road Traffic Acts were yet to come. There was a similar lack of motor vehicle provision, it would seem, for Criminal Investigation Departments, in an era when the villains were as immobile as the police.

Many police forces were also responsible for providing an ambulance service, right up to the start of the Second World War. Here is an example from the Reading force - an Austin ambulance of around 1927, bearing a badge with the words "Reading Borough Police". Note the open cab - something which existed in commercial vehicles much longer than with cars.

Right - In the late-twenties any six-cylinder car was something above the ordinary. This certainly applied to the Morris Six, even though it was based on the popular Oxford model. Deputy Chief Constable Archley of the Warwickshire force was therefore at the right level of seniority to use such a car. It is seen here in the yard of Rugby police station, in about 1929-30.

The 1930s

It was not until the 1930s that the first "patrol cars" were seen on the streets. That is to say, cars were provided to assist in normal policing, whether this was to supervise traffic on important roads or to cover extensive rural areas more efficiently. At that time, though, with the country only beginning to recover from the Depression, economy was the prime consideration. Thus it would have been no surprise to see policemen in MG Midgets, Morris Minors and even Morgan three-wheelers. Some forces even followed a policy of buying their cars second-hand - not without some logic, in an era when depreciation during the first two years of a car's life was even more savage than today.

Nevertheless, during these inter-war years the use of cars was still the exception. Throughout countless films, detective stories and West End plays of that era, the murder was investigated initially by the village sergeant and his constable, who always arrived on bicycles. Only some hours later would the real hero, the chief inspector from the market town, arrive in his car – often driven by another, rather more sophisticated, sergeant. This is in no way to denigrate the village bobby on his bike, who was a symbol of calm and reassurance in rural areas for many decades, but his means of transport was no match for a criminal fraternity which was increasingly becoming motorised.

The specialised needs of policing the nation's roads led to many forces setting up dedicated "motor patrols" in the 1930s. In particular the various Road Traffic Acts created numerous new offences which applied to moving traffic, and the only way to enforce them was to put police constables in cars as well. Not that there was much unanimity about how to go about it. A number of forces thought that a small open sports car offered the best combination of nippiness (from the car) and approachability (on the part of the policemen). Thus we saw MG Midgets and Wolseley Hornets being driven by the men with blue uniforms. Other forces took a

Judging by this photograph, the Buckinghamshire force could claim to have been one of the very first to have established motorised patrols - that is, using cars rather than motorcycles. It shows twelve Morris Cowley two-seaters, clearly just having been delivered, and the date is 1930.

British Police Cars

diametrically opposite route, attracted by a mixture of anonymity and power for their motor patrol vehicles, and found themselves ordering such cars as Ford Model A or Hillman 14 saloons.

One has the feeling that those in charge of motor patrols were privately sad that the car was usurping the horse in this and other aspects of civilised life. Indeed it may well be that Chief Constables were killing two birds with one stone - recognising the need to wind down their forces' equestrian activities and therefore moving the relevant personnel on to the patrol cars. At all events it seems to have been essential for motor patrol crews of the period to wear leather gaiters and gloves, and to stand by their car at all times as if they were holding its reins.

One of the milestones of this period was the formation within the Metropolitan Police of the famous Flying Squad, with its exotic taste in motor cars. Not all of its vehicles were bought new, by any means, but they were uniformly interesting. Who could not be stirred by a combination of Alvis Silver Eagle, Lea-Francis tourer, $4^1/_2$-litre Bentleys, Lagonda saloons and straight-eight

Railtons - not to mention the Beardmore and Morris Commercial taxis?

Another achievement during this time, again involving the "Met", was the setting up of the Driving School at Hendon. It owed its birth to a realisation that police drivers' accident records were so bad as to be indefensible, and that only intensive training could remedy the situation. Hendon became the model for a number of such schools around the country.

Overshadowing the end of the decade, of course, was the ever-increasing threat of war. As in the First World War, every force was going to be depleted by its younger members joining the armed services. To counter this, the authorities would have to make up numbers through the recruitment of "specials" - special constables, who were mostly part-time but who, when on duty, had just the same powers as a regular constable.

Inevitably the looming emergency meant more work for police forces up and down the country. Even before the outbreak of war, numerous orders were being made under the Defence Regulations which still existed as a hangover from World War 1. What was new, however, was a mass of legislation affecting motor vehicles, since

This Humber Snipe tourer of 1930 would have been a prestige model in anyone's hands, let alone those of the Reading police force. It is therefore likely that it is the Chief Constable's car, and that his driver was merely taking a colleague for a ride at the time.

private motoring had hardly been a significant issue during the previous conflict. Apart from the matter of petrol rationing, the most obvious impact of the new regulations was on a car's appearance. All headlamps and driving-lamps had to be severely masked, and - in a feeble attempt to compensate - the edges of wings and running-boards were painted with a white stripe.

Enforcing these and other new rules taxed police resources severely.

The other side of the coin was that, as soon as war was declared and petrol rationing introduced, normal leisure and commuting traffic virtually disappeared. At least one area of police duties - traffic patrols - could therefore be drastically reduced. This was fortunate in a

Staffordshire were using Ford prison vans like this in 1930. This particular one was based at West Bromwich, which these days is part of the West Midlands police area. Note the open cab and small side-windows - still typical for commercial vehicles of those times.

British Police Cars

When in 1930 the Metropolitan Police first started "motor patrols" (as traffic patrols used to be known), they used mainly solo motorcycles and motorcycle combinations. There were some cars as well, including Morris Cowley tourers and the BSA three-wheelers shown here.

An atmospheric shot from about 1931. The Standard Sixteen belongs to the Shropshire force, and is parked in Bridgnorth. A car of this quality is unlikely to have been a mere patrol car; more probably the driver is waiting for someone of chief inspector rank or similar to return.

British Police Cars

way, since car production had also to all intents and purposes closed down. Hence such patrolling as did continue during wartime had to use whatever vehicles were in existence in 1939. Few could have foreseen how long these cars would be asked to go on performing, far beyond the time when they would normally have been replaced. As for those forces that had been economising by following a policy of buying second-hand, they must have looked forward to a long, drawn-out war with more than a little concern.

Left - A Staffordshire County constable, based at West Bromwich, stands beside an Austin Twelve-Four tourer in 1930. No doubt he was the driver, and the car was probably provided for the superintendent of the division. Note the leather gaiters, commonly used as part of drivers' uniforms.

Opposite top - An early example of the Flying Squad's exotic taste in cars - a 1927 4½-litre Bentley tourer which joined their fleet in 1931. One wonders how many times its disreputable-looking crew were pulled over by their own uniformed colleagues, on the grounds that they were an unlikely bunch to be driving such a desirable car.

Right - When the Worcester City force decided in 1931 to introduce motorised patrols, they clearly had economy uppermost in their minds. The choice therefore fell on the Morgan three-wheeler seen here. Possibly they were also influenced by local loyalties, since the car was made only a few miles away in Malvern.

Prison vans, originally horse-drawn, were the first type of police vehicle to become motorised. Otherwise known as "Black Marias", they seem designed to look fearsome. No doubt these two Glasgow vehicles seen in the early-thirties - an Austin Six and a Thorneycroft – were kept busy, especially on Saturday nights.

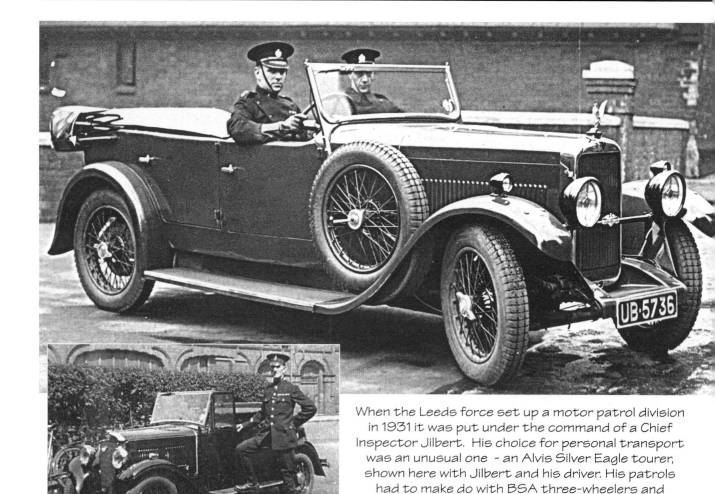

When the Leeds force set up a motor patrol division in 1931 it was put under the command of a Chief Inspector Jilbert. His choice for personal transport was an unusual one - an Alvis Silver Eagle tourer, shown here with Jilbert and his driver. His patrols had to make do with BSA three-wheelers and motorcycle combinations.

Inset left - This Austin 10 drophead coupé of about 1932, of the Reading Borough force, would probably have been used by inspectors going about their area. Note that the driver is wearing riding boots - an affectation of uniform carried over from the days when horse-power was of the four-legged variety.

In the latter part of the last century the Leamington Constabulary was made responsible for the fire service as well. Later it also established the local ambulance service. Here we see the combined garage in 1932. The fire engine on the left is a Leyland, and the ambulance is probably a Dodge.

The press release accompanying this 1932 photo of the "Met's" Ford Model B traffic cars said: "London police on motor patrol are to wear white gauntlets, while on the back window of their cars will be fixed a blind with 'Stop - Police' in large white lettering. This sign will be manipulated by the drivers."

British Police Cars

Prison vans ("Black Marias") did not seem to change much in their design over the years. This Ford version from 1933, belonging to the Metropolitan Police, is shown about to leave Hammersmith Police Station - or so the posed photo would have us believe.

Below - Brand new Morris Isis saloons arrived at the Gloucestershire Constabulary in the summer of 1933. Here they're being proudly shown off by their drivers in front of the headquarters building. One might surmise that the cars were for the use of the Chief Constable and his deputy.

Probably the Flying Squad's most famous car, the Railton Straight Eight saloon of 1933, met their requirements precisely. Railton was one of the first makes to see the merit of a cheap but powerful American engine in a light, sporty chassis. The resultant combination of speed, comfort and relatively low price was just what was needed.

The Reading force were early users of MG Midgets. No doubt they appreciated the combination of performance and manoeuvrability which the cars provided. Shown here is a PA model of 1934, about to go out on traffic patrol. In spite of their compact dimensions the P-type MGs were available in a four-seater version, as seen here.

British Police Cars

Clearly this Wolseley Hornet Special has just been delivered; not only are there important-looking people around in civilian clothes, but the car is wearing trade-plates. It is reputed to have been the first four-wheeled patrol vehicle in the Portsmouth City force - probably around 1935.

Although Ford imported the V8 into Britain as early as 1932, it was only when the company started manufacturing them at Dagenham in 1935 that police forces could contemplate buying the cars. The Gloucestershire force did so immediately; here we see two during a royal visit to Cheltenham Ladies College in that same year.

The Leicester City fleet is shown here, in about 1935. As well as at least one motorcycle combination it contained a 1935 P-Type MG, a 1931 Morris Isis saloon (the Chief Constable's car) and a 1930 Morris Six tourer. Also seen are three vans of various types, which are possibly of Singer manufacture.

Leicestershire's standard-issue patrol car in the mid-thirties was the Austin Ten coupé. Above we see a patrol demonstrating their new 1935 version, complete with open dickey seat. To the left two patrols show off what look like brand-new acquisitions – with the hoods down, of course.

British Police Cars

By 1936, the date this Morris Commercial was first registered, ambulance design had moved forward somewhat. Even so, the Reading Borough force was still responsible for providing the ambulance service in its area. This state of affairs was due to change shortly, however, on the outbreak of war.

An unusual choice as a patrol car in 1936 was the Ford Ten. Gloucestershire acquired three such vehicles in that year, apparently as part of their normal traffic fleet. Here they are shown just after delivery, and presumably before Police signs were added.

Leicestershire County's spanking new pre-war traffic fleet, seen here in 1937, is full of desirable cars. The Jaguars, from 1936 and 1937, are probably the 2½-litre version, while the Wolseleys – all new in 1937 – are likely to be 18/80s. Unfortunately there would be very few new cars for the next ten years.

Police forces up and down the country had a tendency to choose open cars for traffic patrol duties, both before World War 2 and for some years afterwards. Here we see a 1937 Wolseley 14hp tourer belonging to the Metropolitan Police. No doubt the high collars on the uniforms of the time were a help in keeping out the cold.

There has always been a natural affinity between the Bedfordshire force and Vauxhall cars, since the factory lies within the county. In 1937 the traffic fleet seems to have consisted entirely of that marque, made up of Light Six and Twenty-Five saloons as shown here.

31

POLICE

UN 8282

Above - Lancashire showed good taste in traffic cars by ordering one of the desirable MG SA drophead coupés in 1938. The driver, well wrapped up against the cold, is being careful to use the correct hand signal - a lost art in today's motoring.

Although the Daimler saloon shown here was new in 1935, the photo probably dates from somewhat later. The car, run by the Staffordshire force, was probably acquired and converted for loudspeaker use at the time of the Munich crisis in 1938. Note that tyre wear regulations were rather less strict in those days ...

Car maintenance was an integral part of a traffic officer's training in many forces between the wars. Here members of the Staffordshire force receive instruction on a car's inner workings with the help of a sectioned chassis. The photo probably dates from around 1938.

We can probably date this picture of a Metropolitan Police Humber Snipe with some accuracy. The registration was issued in May 1939, and the car certainly looks new. More than that, it sports a single headlamp mask but no white paint, suggesting the era of early wartime regulations in 1939.

British Police Cars

The next stage of wartime car lighting regulations is clearly shown on this Wolseley 14hp saloon, again belonging to the "Met". White paint has been added all round, but there is still only a single headlamp mask. The photo probably dates from 1939; the following year a second headlamp mask would have been added.

First registered in 1938, this Austin Ten was part of the fleet of the Buckinghamshire force – probably a senior officer's transport rather than a traffic car. Once again, the masking of the nearside headlamp suggests that the photo was taken in late-1939.

The 1940s

As in many other areas of life, the development of police motoring effectively came to a standstill for more than half of the forties. Indeed, although it is often convenient to divide up our experience into neat blocks of ten years, the decade we know as "the forties" is really two quite different periods of time - almost two different worlds. Six years of total, all-consuming war came to an abrupt halt in 1945. They were followed by four years of peace, but peace with a price.

By the end of the war the British people, whether they had been overseas with the fighting troops or stayed at home to fight on the economic front, had been through severe privation. Unlike in 1919, however, there were few illusions; there was no talk of "a land fit for heroes". The populace at large knew that the economic cost had been severe, that the British Empire had either been lost or was about to be, and that it would need some considerable time to regain even the standard of living they had enjoyed in the late-thirties.

Gradually industry picked up where it had left off in 1939. The motor industry was in a particularly weak state. Unlike many areas of engineering, it had been

Although this converted Dennis bus was originally registered in 1924, the picture seems to date from early World War 2; note the headlamp mask and white paint on wings and running-boards. Since it belonged to the Portsmouth City force, we can assume that it was of particular use in emergencies such as air raids.

given little opportunity to develop new products and techniques during wartime. Yet in spite of this it was singled out to spearhead the country's export effort, in a frenzied attempt to earn foreign exchange, particularly dollars. The vast fabric of wartime controls was kept in place and used to enforce this policy - for example by relating a company's allocation of steel to its success in gaining export sales.

Unsurprisingly, most car manufacturers elected to resume the production of pre-war models as fast as possible, and to relegate new model development to a low priority for the time being. Worse, from the point of view of the British motorist, was the realisation that as much of this production as possible was heading for export, leaving the home market in a state of severe starvation. The resultant "grey market" which developed is worthy of a separate book in itself.

Chief Constables were left to work out for themselves what they should do about their fleets. No doubt some could call in favours and get hold of new cars rather more quickly than the average private buyer. But was it worth it, when all you finished up with was a Hillman Minx or Wolseley 14 which was indistinguishable from the one you had bought in 1938?

British Police Cars

Although some forces had women on their strength during the twenties and thirties, the recruitment of female police officers received a major boost during World War 2 with the formation of the Women's Auxiliary Police Corps. Here are two of them, in about 1942, trying to start an Armstrong-Siddeley of the Leicestershire fleet with its starting handle.

And moreover the 1938 car in many cases had covered such a small mileage during the war years that it still had plenty of life left in it.

Gradually new models, albeit closely related to pre-war ones, began to appear. The Austin 16, to name but one example, was a favourite amongst a number of police forces in the late forties. The attractively-styled Riley 2½-litre also became a popular choice. And a sign of things to come was when the new Jaguar Mk V saloon, launched in 1948, began to be chosen for service.

Even so, many forces continued to run their pre-war cars. Replacement of their fleets must have been hard to justify, given that private motoring was still severely curtailed by petrol rationing. In many ways the post-war motoring scene was a time-warp, with the majority of private cars, police cars and even vans and lorries having been manufactured in the thirties, and the remainder resembling them so much that it was hard to tell the difference. Even the roads had hardly altered - once the signposts, removed during the war, bad been put back in place.

Some changes were coming about. Wireless, still experimental in the thirties, had become much more reliable as a result of wartime development. It began to be adopted by most forces, although initially only in a restricted number of cars. The "area wireless car" was the equivalent of today's rapid response vehicle, since it could be located immediately and given a new assignment. An alternative method of communicating with mobile patrols which was used at this period is hard to credit nowadays: the nearest local police stations or country beat houses were given a message by phone, and then called the car in by hanging a disc outside their premises.

The need for a more rapid response was intensified by the wider availability of private telephones, and by the way that the public was encouraged to use them. Importantly, a new emergency code was introduced nationwide - the "999" system. Although it had been adopted in the late-thirties in the Metropolitan Police area, other parts of the country still relied on dialling "0" for the operator and taking their chances with all the other calls waiting for long-distance connections. The 999 number, launched in what in those days passed for a blaze of publicity, allowed the

How this London-registered 1938 Ford V8 managed to turn up in the Hampshire fleet is anyone's guess. This particular model is comparatively rare, only some 1200 having been built at Dagenham. The headlamp masks date the photo at some time in the latter part of the Second World War – say, 1943-44.

British Police Cars

operator to give instant attention to an emergency call.

Gradually other changes asserted themselves. The petrol allocation for private motoring was steadily increased, followed in 1950 by the total abolition of rationing. The number of motorists, and their annual mileage, soared in response. In consequence the policing and control of traffic started to become a major part of a police force's responsibilities. It was during this period, therefore, that most forces formed separate traffic sections, with their own command structure.

It was inevitable that these new traffic sections would perceive the need to have more specialised vehicles than they had been given previously. In the late forties, we can begin to see some of the influence of this new thinking. Cars with higher performance, in either straight-line terms or in their roadholding, began to appear. Some examples we have already mentioned - the RM-Series Rileys, and the Mark V Jaguar. The choice of this latter model resulted from another emerging requirement, which was for more space for equipment. Both these needs would become ever more important in the ensuing decades.

With the war over in 1946 we see yet another of the Metropolitan Police's much-loved Wolseley saloons, here driving into Scotland Yard. This model is probably the new version of the 14 - virtually identical to the pre-war model but with a slight increase in power.

Sports cars retained their popularity as traffic patrol cars after World War 2 – understandably, as they were agile enough to negotiate the slow traffic on Britain's narrow roads. Here a batch of six MG TCs are seen at MG's Abingdon factory, being collected by their Warwickshire drivers. The date is early in 1946.

British Police Cars

Left - Here we can see one of the Warwickshire MG TCs from the earlier picture, ready to go out on patrol. Note that the car has now been fitted with police signs front and rear and a loudspeaker. The crew is clearly looking forward to its shift on a fine summer's day, but it must have been a cold job in winter.

Right - Oxford City was another force which seemed to appreciate the attractions of MG Midgets as traffic cars. No doubt they were well aware that the cars were made just outside their boundary, in Abingdon. This shot from about 1946 shows an early TC model crossing Magdalen bridge in Oxford. Note the outsize auxiliary horn.

Left - Proof of the way in which pre-war police fleets had their lives extended during and after World War 2. Half of the Worcestershire cars lined up in 1946 – one of the Humber Super Snipes and both the Wolseley 18s – date from 1938/39, and are still in use seven or eight years later. The other three – two Humbers and the Austin 16 – are very recent acquisitions.

Like a number of other forces, Gloucestershire was interested in the post-war Riley 2½-litre saloon. It would seem that they bought one first for evaluation, for we see here two officers from the force picking up such a car – still on trade-plates - from the Riley works in Coventry, probably in 1946.

British Police Cars

Right - In 1947 the Warwickshire force took delivery of five new Austin 16 patrol cars (one per division). Here they're being handed over by the supplying garage in Nuneaton. The Austin 16 was a popular choice with many police forces; these five were not the only ones operated by Warwickshire, as we shall see.

Left - Did this 1947 photo depict yet another staged incident for the benefit of the photographer, or was it a real one? The Wolseley (is it an 18/85 model?) and the motorcycles are part of a Metropolitan Police "traffic accident group", apparently interrogating the driver of an elderly Armstrong-Siddeley in Hyde Park.

Right - Nottingham City police made an unusual choice in 1947, supplying their patrols with Bedford vans. However the vehicles had also undergone the Martin Walter "Utilecon" conversion, effectively making them estate cars. Here we see the fleet of eight being inspected, presumably just after delivery.

Gloucestershire's evaluation of the 2½-litre Riley (see page 41) seems to have been positive. Here is the proof – the whole traffic fleet, consisting of no less than ten of these cars, pictured in the spring of 1947. The RM-series Rileys were popular amongst a number of forces.

Although this heavy load is being escorted through Stafford by a Staffordshire traffic car of pre-war origin, the event in fact occurred after the war - probably around 1948. If proof is needed, the Diamond T tractors are left-hand drive and clearly ex-US Army. The Austin 14 was new in 1938 and had thus remained in service for some ten years.

British Police Cars

In the post-war years Humbers had nearly as much attraction as Wolseleys as the favoured marque for police fleets. Here we see a Snipe in about 1948, in use by an inspector of the Bedfordshire force. This particular car looks less like part of the traffic fleet and more like a senior officer's car.

The pre-war Hillman 14 was a larger, more robust car than the Minx, but less expensive than the equivalent Humber. The Warwickshire force appears to have acquired this car new and then run it all through the war, since this now somewhat fogged photo was taken in about 1948. Interestingly, the registration number has been retained from an even older car - why?

A Humber Snipe area wireless car of the Metropolitan Police speeds on its way to an emergency, helped by a uniformed colleague stopping the traffic. At this period (around 1948) radio was far from a universal installation in police cars, either in the "Met" or elsewhere.

It seems that the Leicester City Constabulary had a problem with pickpockets in the city centre at some time in 1949. The detective constable's solution was apparently to photograph them in the act. Note that he has allayed their suspicions by removing the "Police" sign from the car.

British Police Cars

We have already seen the Warwickshire force taking delivery of five of these same cars, Austin 16s, in 1947. This particular one, from its number plate, must have been delivered before then, but it is still in service some time later - probably around 1949 (note that the uniform has changed). If the other five were divisional cars, then possibly this was a senior officer's car.

How the "Met" loved their Wolseleys! This one appears to be the 18/85 model, often used for traffic patrol work. The surroundings, and the presence of the two motorcycles, suggest that the photo was taken near the Hendon police driving school, probably on a training run in about 1949.

The 1950s

In contrast to the rather austere forties, the decade of the fifties was one of ever-increasing prosperity for the British people. The occasional setback, such as the increase in commodity prices brought on by the Korean War, was no more than a blip in a steady upward trend in the standard of living. People's attitudes changed slowly but surely throughout the decade. At the beginning, still emerging from the regimentation of wartime, they showed a kind of meek acceptance of their lot. By 1959, the mood had changed dramatically to one of near-triumphalism - immortalised by Prime Minister Harold Macmillan in that year's election, when he told the British people "you've never had it so good".

In many ways the fifties were the calm before the storm. As well as rising standards of living and low unemployment, there was less unrest amongst the nation as a whole, either in industry or on the streets. It was probably the last decade of conformism - when the younger generation, in general, aspired to be like their parents rather than to be as different as possible. For the police, therefore, it was probably the last period when their law-enforcement was accepted without question by the majority of the population.

The British motor industry seemed to be part of this rather complacent pattern. The initial surge of post-war demand for cars had been satisfied, but increased prosperity had ensured that the car factories remained at full stretch. With the advantage of hindsight, though, one can see that below the surface all was not well. Vast though it was, the motor industry remained composed of far too many small, inefficient units, producing under-researched models which were increasingly being judged as uncompetitive in export markets around the world. The only exceptions to this dismal judgement were the two American-owned companies - Ford and Vauxhall.

Jaguars were used after the Second World War, and well before the Mark 2 and XJ6 models became so popular. Their predecessors, the E-Type coupé and the Mark 7 saloon, were used by some forces. Here we see an even earlier Jaguar, the Mark 5 saloon, photographed outside the headquarters of the Warwickshire force in around 1950.

British Police Cars

Nevertheless the British motorist continued to be satisfied with his home country's products, especially as import tariffs made any imported competition look expensive by comparison. And naturally enough the same went for the country's police forces, who had no reason not to buy the same kinds of car. What did begin to emerge, though, was a strengthening of the trend we noted at the end of the forties. To keep up with the nation's traffic, and also to haul around an increasing amount of equipment, their cars had to be bigger, more powerful, and just plain faster.

This was of course particularly applicable to traffic patrol vehicles. It is noticeable that the cars selected around the country were frequently of the same makes as before, but were upgraded in size and power. Often it would be the six-cylinder elder brother of the four-cylinder model chosen previously. Thus we see the Vauxhall Velox replacing the Wyvern, the Austin Westminster usurping the Hampshire, and so on. The Wolseley 6/90 was a godsend to many forces, allowing them to maintain their loyalty to Wolseley and yet employ a powerful six-cylinder saloon of relatively modern design. This perceived need for six cylinders also allowed Ford to start making inroads into the market, with its first Zephyr Six model.

The amount of paraphernalia which had to be carried around was at least as important a factor as sheer speed in influencing the choice of car. One of the

The post-war RM-type Riley was appreciated by many forces for its all-round abilities. Good roadholding was common to all models in this series, but in the bigger-engined 2½-litre model it was coupled with particularly good performance. Here a Portsmouth City 2½-litre RMB model from around 1950 is shown at speed.

most frequent tasks, then as now, for a patrol was to control the flow of traffic after an accident. As speeds and traffic densities rose, it demanded an increasingly sophisticated approach which involved both intensive training and specialised equipment such as sign-boards and lighting (the now-ubiquitous traffic cone had not yet arrived). One solution, often tried since, was to use an estate car. Estate car variants of saloons were less common then than now, but one which filled the bill admirably was the Humber Super Snipe.

Another additional load to be carried was the radio receiver-transmitter. Whereas a few years previously this had only been fitted to a minority of cars, it was now regarded as essential equipment for both traffic and area cars. With the transistor still in the laboratory, the valve-operated sets of the time were both heavy and bulky. Many cars were also fitted with public address equipment, which was much heavier than today's equivalent.

As far as area cars were concerned there seems to have been little agreement on an ideal model, and individual forces as usual went out and bought what

A similar Portsmouth Riley to the one pictured on the previous page is proudly shown off by mechanics from the police garage. Mechanics have always been the unsung heroes; drivers depending on them to keep their cars on the road.

British Police Cars

appealed to them. Wolseleys, of course, were not unknown - the 4/50 and the 4/44 being the models usually chosen. Humber Hawks appeared here and there, as did Austin A70s, Hillman Minxes and Ford Consuls.

It was only later in the decade that an event occurred which would have a major impact on traffic sections throughout the country. This was the opening of Britain's first motorway - not the M1, as is often supposed, but the Preston bypass. This short section of what was to become the M6 opened in December 1958, with the initial stretch of the M1 following in 1959. So Britain's motorists suddenly had nearly seventy miles of

an entirely new sort of road on which to test their skills - with no speed limit, at least for the first few years.

Policing of the new motorways, divided amongst the forces' areas through which they passed, focussed even more attention on traffic sections and their equipment. Cars which had to travel at motorway speeds for day after day, night after night, had to be more robust and more reliable than ever before. Visibility would be important, too - that is, a stationary police car on the hard shoulder had to be easily visible to the fast-moving traffic approaching it. These factors soon began to have an important influence on the types of car which traffic sections preferred to use.

The traffic section of the Blackpool force was another to favour the Humber Super Snipe in the early post-war years. This summer-time snap dates from about 1950. Note that by this date the Blackpool uniform had changed from the high-collar type to the lapel type.

The Malvern division of the Worcestershire force had this Humber Hawk allocated to it in 1951. Although many forces had a continuing love affair with the Humber marque, this particular vehicle is in some ways a surprising choice; the early post-war Hawks with their side-valve engines were usually regarded as somewhat underpowered.

It is difficult to say whether these Leicestershire and Rutland Austin A40s of 1951 are the "Countryman" estate model or vans. Since their roofs appear to have been modified (to take the radio aerials?) however, the latter seems more likely.

British Police Cars

Right - The Leicestershire force, now known after an amalgamation as the Leicestershire and Rutland Constabulary, converted this Austin Freeway van in 1951 for use as a mobile police station.

Above - The Jaguar Mark VII saloon was a relevation when it was announced in 1950. Its 3.4-litre twin-overhead cam engine had already achieved fame in the XK120 sports car of two years earlier. Worcestershire were impressed by the model, and acquired two in 1952 – this is one of them.

Right - Between the essentially pre-war 14 and 18hp models and the much more modern 6/90, Wolseley managed to retain its sales to police forces with the 6/80, which was basically an uprated Morris Six. The restored example shown here, dating from 1951, was operated by the Swansea force.

Ford's range of six-cylinder cars.- Zephyrs and Granadas - were a familiar sight in police livery for many years. One of the first forces to use them was Staffordshire, which put the first Zephyr Six model into service when it was launched in 1951. This photo dates from 1953.

British Police Cars

How many forces managed to keep a car going for sixteen years? This Ford V8 "woody" estate was new in 1937, but was still in service with the Hampshire force when this shot was taken in about 1953. Note that as well as having three separate loudspeakers the car is fitted with a siren rather than the "gong" - a very early application.

The E-series Vauxhall Velox, launched in 1951, was a much more modern design than its predecessor. Importantly it at last had a full-width body, which gave it more generous interior dimensions. Here we see a 1954 version, in service as a patrol car with the Worcestershire County force.

A Nottinghamshire Austin A70 Hereford pictured in the winter of 1954, while in service as a divisional area car. Area cars probably had as hard a life as the traffic cars, since they had to be used on a far greater variety of roads - often with much inferior surfaces.

Sussex was another force which operated Rileys in the fifties. This example is not pictured smartly turned out for nothing: the crew are awaiting their Chief Constable's annual inspection in 1954. The equipment on display is minimal compared with the amount which a modern patrol would carry.

British Police Cars

Left - Gloucestershire remained loyal to the Riley marque even when the RM-series models had been replaced. The new model was the Pathfinder – admittedly sharing its body with the Wolseley 6/90, but at least retaining the traditional twin-camshaft Riley engine. The driver shown here seems pleased with his "office".

Opposite bottom - In 1954 Wolseley updated its range by replacing the 6/80 model with a totally new one - the 6/90. The Metropolitan force, faithful as ever to the Wolseley marque, purchased some for traffic patrol work. The example shown here dates from 1956.

Below - The Worcestershire force updated its motor patrol fleet significantly in the period 1954-55. The two Mark VII Jaguars acquired earlier were joined by a third, and to these were added six Vauxhall Veloxes. Shown here is the full fleet in about 1956, lined up in front of what were then the relatively new headquarters at Hindlip Hall. Note that in this case the uniforms have still not changed to the lapel type.

Left - Part of the Oxfordshire fleet in 1955 seems to show a new delivery of all-Austin vehicles. The traffic cars are A50 Cambridges, while at the back A40 Countryman estates are for the dog section. Here Oxfordshire traffic section has adopted the white-topped cap but not yet the chequered band.

British Police Cars

Although Bedfordshire is the home of the Vauxhall factory, this did not stop the county force using rival products when it suited it. In 1956, for instance – before the arrival of motorways – their preferred vehicle for trunk road patrols was the Zephyr Six, as shown here.

Below - When in 1956 Austin updated the previous A90 six-cylinder model to become the A95, they gave it more power and a much bigger boot. The Metropolitan Police force added the new model to its traffic patrol fleet and kept it in operation for some years thereafter, until it was replaced by the A99.

The Cornwall force was another impressed by the new Austin A95 when it was announced in 1956; they added two examples to their fleet in early 1957. Here we see them, accompanied by an Austin A70 Hereford and a Bedford van, at the force's centenary celebrations in Bodmin the same year.

Inset - Many forces other than the "Met" were faithful to the Wolseley marque, for reasons which, today, are hard to understand. The more modern lines of the new 6/90 model would have been welcomed by the numerous forces operating them. One such force was Southampton, which ran the 1957 model shown here.

British Police Cars

Right - When in 1959 they took over responsibility for patrolling part of the new M1 motorway, Bedfordshire traffic section decided that their cars had to be more visible. They therefore ordered their new Ford Farnham estate cars to be painted entirely in white (they claim they were the first force to do so). The blue roof light was also an innovation.

In 1959 the Stockport Borough force was running a whole fleet of General Motors vehicles - Vauxhalls and Bedfords. Area cars were Wyverns, vans were Bedfords, and the traffic cars were PA Veloxes, as shown here.

The 1960s

After the relatively calm fifties, the next decade was one almost of turbulence for Britain's police forces, and particularly as far as their vehicles were concerned. Major changes embraced both traffic sections and regular beat patrolling. At the same time the police forces themselves, under pressure to increase efficiency, were undergoing profound organisational change.

The first influence - the motorway building programme - was already under way at the start of the sixties. During the decade of the 1960s, however, many more county forces had to come to terms with a motorway existing within their boundaries, with all that this meant in terms of policing. The traffic section's training, procedures and vehicles all had to be adapted to the requirements of patrolling these new high-speed roads.

Many forces felt that the need to have vehicles of sufficient speed was paramount. This was particularly true in the first few years, when there was no legal speed limit on

When Austin's latest Westminster model – the A99 – was announced in 1959, its improvements over the previous A95 version were very enticing. As well as its greater interior space and increased power, it boasted disc brakes in front. The Worcestershire force acquired this particular car early in 1960.

motorways (or indeed on most roads outside built-up areas). Even after 1965, when the 70mph limit was first imposed, motorways were still judged to be the place where high-speed pursuits were most likely to take place. Thus we saw such high-performance cars as the Jaguar E-Type or the Sunbeam Tiger being brought into service.

Inevitably, though, the question of sheer carrying capacity began to predominate. An E-Type Jaguar coupé, desirable vehicle though it was, could never hold as much equipment as a saloon. And even if it could, the effect on its overall weight would bring its performance down to that of the equivalent saloon. It was probably arguments such as these which saw most forces tending more and more towards high-performance saloons for their motorway patrols. This was the era when the smaller Jaguar saloons were most often seen -

particularly the Mk2 3.8, and later the S-Type. Other popular choices were Ford Zephyr Sixes and the Austin/Wolseley A99 or 6/99 range (later A110 and 6/110).

British Police Cars

Another feature which tends to distinguish the sixties from the fifties is the colour in which police vehicles were painted. As far as traffic cars were concerned, motorways brought a new requirement - the need to be seen at all times. When a car was stopped on the hard shoulder at night, or in fog, a flashing blue light was not sufficient to ensure that it could be seen. Exactly which force was the first to paint its vehicles white is a matter for debate, but by the mid-sixties it had become the common colour for motorway patrols.

Meanwhile, away from the world of traffic patrols, a revolution was under way for the beat policeman. "Unit Beat Policing" was seen as the way forward in the sixties, and it meant removing men from the beat and putting them in the strangely-named Panda Cars instead. A panda car was a small, agile vehicle which could slip easily through city streets and respond quickly to a call from the public. Typically in those days it would be an Austin 1300, a Ford Escort, a Morris Minor or a Vauxhall Viva. As with their motorway counterparts, the cars were painted in a distinctive colour scheme, so that they would stand out from normal traffic.

Once Unit Beat Policing had been introduced, certain disadvantages became apparent. Importantly, the system was seen to distance the police constable from the public at large, members of which could no longer see policemen physically on the streets. This went down badly with both the public and beat policemen (and women) themselves, and the system had to be heavily modified. Even so, the panda car name remained and has become part of our language.

The 1960s was a period in which another revolution was taking place - the amalgamation of smaller police forces into much larger ones. The trend had been there since the early days of policing, with the smaller towns giving up control of their tiny numbers to the relevant

Even in the fifties the radio equipment fitted to patrol cars could not give wholly reliable reception. In the right type of operation, therefore, a specialist communications vehicle like this 1960 Ford Thames van of the Leicestershire and Rutland force could be a great help.

county forces. However the larger "County Boroughs" were more jealous of their independence, and it took some compulsion from the Home Office to make such places see the advantages of a force covering a larger area. From the point of view of a car enthusiast, however, something was lost. Previously each force had followed its own purchasing policy, which had resulted in an amazing range of makes and models bearing blue-and-white police signs.

The creation of the new larger forces also coincided with a period of consolidation in the British motor industry. Mergers and model rationalisation - long overdue, many would say - resulted in a far more limited choice in any one price class. Up to then, of

Above - The Jaguar Mk 2 saloon, particularly in 3.8-engined form as shown here, was one of the finest traffic cars of its time. This 1960 example was operated by the Buckinghamshire force, which later became one of the constituents of the Thames Valley amalgamation.

Humbers were long favoured by the Metropolitan Police, and the new Super Snipe estate met their needs for a traffic car perfectly. It offered a superb combination for the time of comfort, space and performance. This example is pictured after delivery in about 1960.

British Police Cars

A "Met" Humber Super Snipe estate is seen once again, in the Lambeth area, this time showing off the extent of the equipment it can carry. With it is a Daimler SP250 sports, a model which the same force used extensively during the sixties.

course, it had been assumed that a British force would buy British-made cars. However the Chief Constables of these new forces were motivated much more by considerations of efficiency than by sentiment, and some began to think the unthinkable ... It was not only a matter of price and performance; the important question of reliability was also an issue. Unfortunately the British motor industry was entering its most infamous period, and its products were starting to earn themselves an unenviable reputation in matters of both design and reliability.

When Hampshire took the plunge in 1965 and became the first force to go "foreign" (they bought Volvo 121 estates), the cries of protest could be heard all over the land. Yet within a very few years the hubbub had died down and it became a common sight to see BMWs, Volvos and many other imported makes in police livery. And who could not accept this situation, when it merely mirrored what was happening in the car market as a whole? Although the trend was to accelerate in the seventies, the late-sixties saw imports starting to increase their share of the total market. The private buyer, in other words, was beginning to use the same logical reasons for buying his new car as Chief Constables were.

Who can doubt the appeal of the Jaguar as a traffic car when they see a line-up like this one? At the time (1960) Bedfordshire was using a mixture of Mark 1s and Mark 2s. Interestingly, unlike the Farnham estates they have not been specified in white.

British Police Cars

The Leicestershire and Rutland traffic division took delivery of these Mk 2 Jaguars in late-1961. Note that this force too has adopted white livery and roof-lamps. Presumably the dark-coloured Mark IX Jaguar is the Chief Constable's car.

Right - A fine 1961 action shot of a Metropolitan Police Daimler SP 250 on its way back to the Hendon police driving school. Although there were some misgivings about this model's fibre-glass body, there was universal praise for its Edward Turner-designed V8 engine - which was later fitted to a version of the Mk 2 Jaguar.

Lancashire traffic section ran an interesting combination of vehicles in 1962, as illustrated here. Their drivers had a choice of comfort, provided by the Mk2 Ford Zephyr estate, or fresh air, represented by the MGA. These two very different cars had remarkably similar performance.

By 1962 Leicestershire had added the Ford Zephyr Six to its traffic fleet. Note that it was now normal to specify white livery and blue roof-lamps. This was the model which became widely known as the "Z-Car" after the popular television series.

British Police Cars

Anyone who was on traffic patrol in the infamous winter of 1963 will not forget it in a hurry! The Austin A99 Westminster of the Gloucestershire force shown here can only just pass through the track made by a snow-plough. Gloucestershire purchased a number of these cars.

Above - Humber changed its image overnight when it scrapped its long-lasting post-war Hawk model in 1957. The new models with their full-width bodies found immediate favour in a number of forces, including Cardiff City which ran the 1963 Series III pictured here.

An Austin 1100 of the Oxford City force patrols the city at dusk in about 1963. This is probably an area car rather than part of the traffic section, but it pre-dates the introduction of panda cars.

By 1963, when this picture was taken, MG had replaced the MGA model with the MGB. The Metropolitan Police decided to try out the new car for traffic patrol work. Here it is shown with an all-woman crew - the first time this had happened in the "Met".

106 FLY

British Police Cars

As far as police forces were concerned, the Ford Zephyr Mark 3 range carried on where the Mark 2 left off. Amongst other things, these cars offered unbeatable value-for-money. This Warwickshire Zephyr is seen at the Royal Show at Stoneleigh, probably in 1964. Also in attendance are members of the mounted section of the Birmingham force.

Here is the same Humber Super Snipe estate which we saw earlier (pages 63 & 64) just after it had been delivered to the Metropolitan Police. By the time this picture was taken, some time around 1963, it was operating as part of an accident prevention unit.

The Ford Corsair filled a niche above the Cortina but below the Zephyr. It marked the first use of Ford's V4 engine, also to become familiar in the Transit van. This Corsair from 1965 was used as a divisional area car in the Cheshire force.

Below - This is the car that started a revolution in police forces throughout the country. In 1965 the Hampshire force decided that the British motor industry no longer produced a suitable car for their traffic patrolling needs. They therefore bought Volvo 121 estates, causing howls of anguish amongst traditionalists.

British Police Cars

Another force which liked the Mk2 Jaguar was Staffordshire, which used the model particularly for patrolling the section of the M6 which passes through its county. The four shown here were delivered in January 1965. By now motorway cars were painted white as a matter of course.

Before "panda cars" and "unit beat policing" there were earlier experiments in motorising the beat policeman. In 1965 these Stockport Morris Minor 1000s were known as "courtesy and advice" cars. Whether the stripes served to attract the public's attention or to frighten them is not recorded ...

Within the Ford range the Cortina was less often seen in police forces compared with its six-cylinder brethren. This Bedfordshire Cortina Super from 1965 is clearly not employed on traffic duties, and is likely to have been, say, a sergeant's supervisory car.

Wolseleys continued to hold their attraction for police forces well into the sixties. The 6/90 model was superseded by the bigger and more powerful 6/99. Once again, the Metropolitan Police ordered some of the new model. This 1965 example is shown on duty in Trafalgar Square.

British Police Cars

The idea of you and your car being stopped merely for a roadside check was something new in 1965. In Leicestershire and Rutland it was judged to require some press publicity in order to explain to the public what was going on. The result was this posed shot of a Rutland County Mk2 Jaguar crew interviewing the driver of a Riley 4/72.

The "Met" photographers had a liking for staged shots such as this one from around 1967. Shown are a Jaguar S-Type saloon from the traffic section, a Ford Anglia panda car and an Austin Mini van being used by the dog section.

Left - A Jaguar E-Type coupé operated by the Berkshire force peels off the M4 motorway in 1966. No other car of similar price could come near this model for sheer performance, but it was somewhat deficient as regards carrying capacity - even with the extra nine inches of the 2+2 model, which this one appears to be.

The Austin A110 Westminster was in use for a number of years amongst many police forces. Here we see a Warwickshire traffic patrol away from its usual A-road routes, and instead making its way gingerly down The Parade at Leamington. The date is probably early in 1967.

British Police Cars

Above - When the unit beat system was introduced nationally in 1967, there was inevitable nostalgia for the disappearance of the old ways. Here an obviously posed photo seems designed to bring tears to our eyes, as the Bedfordshire constable learns that his bicycle has been made obsolete by a Mini.

Top right - As an alternative to panda cars, many forces decided on estate cars or vans for their more rural beats. Here we see a Morris 1000 van being used in this way by the Cumbria force in 1967.

Unit beat policing was in its infancy when this 1967 shot was taken. The Ford Anglia, here belonging to the Lancashire force, was a popular choice as a panda car. Radio technology at the time demanded that the constable's personal radio worked via the car's transmitter/receiver.

When the panda system was introduced in 1967, Vauxhall must have been glad that its local force, Bedfordshire, chose the Viva for its rural patrols. The force promptly commissioned a series of publicity photos to celebrate – as in this posed shot of a patrol officer at a farm in the north of the county.

1967 was a record year for purchases of police cars, thanks to the introduction of unit beat policing. The Worcestershire County force settled on the Morris Mini Traveller as its panda car. This model had an attractive specification, offering superb manoeuvrability with reasonable carrying capacity. Here we see five of them after delivery.

British Police Cars

The ever-increasing number of vehicles, especially after the introduction of panda cars, meant that police forces had to upgrade and expand their workshop facilities. Here we see the Lancashire police workshops hard at work in 1967.

Reading's first panda cars, ten Vauxhall Vivas, seen lined up after delivery in late-1967. Here the "unit beat" system replaced one that had involved individual beat officers on motorcycles. The new system, introduced all over the country, had to be modified after complaints from the public.

Local loyalties took a long time to die out in some areas. It would not strike everyone that the Hillman Imp was an ideal traffic car. Nevertheless the Dumbartonshire force decided on that model in 1967. The car was made in nearby Linwood ...

British Police Cars

One of the 1967 Worcestershire panda fleet of Mini Travellers seen previously, is shown here supposedly in use. At this stage panda car drivers kept their normal helmets, to maintain their connection in the public's mind with the beat policeman.

Sunbeam's Tiger was a high-powered version of the Alpine sports car, with an American Ford V8 engine shoe-horned in. The resultant heady mix of power and agility was too much for some police forces to resist. Shown here is a Metropolitan Police traffic patrol in around 1967.

Yet another force prepares for the novelty of unit beat policing. These two-door Austin 1100 Mk2s were Gloucestershire's solution to the new system. The theory was that constables would go out to a central point and from there walk their beat – but for many the driving was more attractive than the walking.

The Ford Cortina Mk2 may not have been an obvious traffic car, although it was surprisingly roomy. However in GT form it also became a spirited performer. The Essex force obviously appreciated its qualities, as shown by their car in action here.

British Police Cars

The Austin 1800 range had its attractions for traffic work, since it offered huge interior space for what was essentially a medium-size car. This was of course a result of the transverse positioning of its engine, following on from the Mini and 1100/1300 models.

Below - Another shot of the Staffordshire Austin 1800, leading a line of cars out of the Stafford headquarters on a training run in about 1968. Although this force was running Mk2 Jaguars for motorway patrols, there were different models - apparently all Austins - in use for other traffic work, such as A110 Westminsters and the smaller A60.

An alternative to a saloon car for the unit beat system was a small estate car, with its increased carrying capacity for equipment. The Edinburgh City force went in this direction, and decided on the Morris Minor 1000 Traveller. One of the Edinburgh cars is shown in this shot from around 1968.

One aspect of traffic work which receives little publicity is the question of driver training. After the "Met" set up their driver training school at Hendon in 1934, certain other police forces round the country did likewise. Here we see an unmarked Austin 1800 from the Staffordshire school involved in some discreet training in about 1967.

British Police Cars

A lonely Staffordshire panda car is photographed on a bright snowy day on rural patrol. Whatever the limitations of the "unit beat" system, it certainly allowed patrolling in areas that otherwise tended to be ignored. The location is Cannock Chase, and the date 1968.

Staffordshire renewed their motorway patrol fleet in early-1969, and again chose Jaguars – this time the 340, successor to the Mk2. Here the cars are lined up just after delivery. It would appear that in the intervening four years the decision had been taken to increase the size of the fleet from four to six.

The 1970s

Is it too early to become nostalgic about the seventies? For some of us it probably is; especially those who were involved in some way or the other with the British motor industry and whose memories are bitter-sweet at best. This was the decade when the shortcomings of that industry – and of many others – were all too cruelly exposed to the realities of international competition. During virtually the whole post-war period, Britain had been living in something of a dream world, and it took the shocks of the seventies to open the eyes of the British people to the real situation.

For the car buyer, too, the

A Rover V8 3500 of the Thames Valley force is seen on patrol in 1970. This model proved ideal for traffic sections and was deservedly popular. It offered an attractive combination of space and comfort coupled with excellent performance.

seventies were a decade of awakening. Even if he managed to remain ignorant of the industry's problems, he could hardly fail to notice that his new car was often delivered much later than had been promised, and that thereafter it was not very reliable. He (or, increasingly, she) might also have noticed that there were many more imported cars on the roads, and that they seemed to be highly competitive in every area – price, quality,

delivery, reliability and so on. This was due as much as anything to the reduction in import duties which had begun in the sixties and accelerated in the following ten years. Naturally police forces recognised these things just as much as the public, and the trend to imported cars – BMWs, for example - became more noticeable.

Where nostalgia does play a part, however, is in the loss of so many famous names which had adorned the radiators of police cars over the years. Even before the seventies had started, the Riley marque had disappeared. During the decade there was an even bigger loss, when the Wolseley name went. Wolseley had lost its way before then, its last model being a mid-size BMC saloon with a six-cylinder engine squeezed in crossways. At the same time Austin, for many years a police favourite, no longer produced the larger cars needed for traffic work. Under the new British Leyland regime the Austin marque had to concede this market to Triumph, Rover and Jaguar. These three names were later reduced to two when the six-cylinder Triumph saloons were dropped.

British Police Cars

It was the same story in what had been the Rootes group, taken over by Chrysler during the sixties. By the start of the seventies the large Humbers – for so long favoured by police forces – had disappeared, and the Humber name was confined to a variant of the four-cylinder Hillman Minx. The Singer marque had disappeared altogether before the start of the decade, and by its end Sunbeam had almost done the same.

Even more surprising was the way in which Vauxhall gave up its claim to this same market for most of the seventies. Previously its six-cylinder Velox/Cresta range had been seized on by more than one police force as fulfilling its requirements. Now there was nothing above the mid-size Victor (later the Cavalier) - not until the company eventually imported the Opel Senator and rebadged it as the Royale.

Nevertheless, amongst the makes and models which were left there were some surprisingly good ones.

Yet another variation on the "sports car with a big engine" formula was the MGC, which squeezed the big six-cylinder engine from the Austin-Healey into the space previously occupied by an 1800cc B-Series four-cylinder unit. The Metropolitan force were attracted, and added the model to their traffic fleet in 1970.

Jaguar had not long before (1968) launched its sensational XJ6 model, Rover fitted a V8 engine into the P6 bodyshell to produce the 3500, and in 1972 Ford replaced the unloved Zodiac Mark 4 with the Granada. Notwithstanding the usual seventies problems of delivery, quality and reliability, all these cars were fine designs which gave good service to police forces and private buyers alike.

As a prime example of a seventies car suited to police work, perhaps one should single out the Rover 3500. Its all-aluminium Buick-designed V8 engine was already well-known, having been used in the P5 3.5-Litre model since 1967. A year later it was fitted into the lighter body, and the resulting gain in performance at once attracted the attention of motoring enthusiasts, not to mention police forces. By the start of the seventies the Rover 3500 was well established in a number of forces, and they continued to re-order the model until it was superseded in 1977.

A number of forces found the Ford Cortina Mk2 a useful traffic car, although usually for non-motorway work. Here we see one belonging to the Buckinghamshire force being serviced in their workshops in about 1970. The vehicle inside on the lift appears to be a Range Rover, apparently not part of the traffic section's fleet.

The Granada was another widely-used model, together with its close relation the Consul GT (effectively a Mark 1 Granada without the vinyl roof). Compared with the Zodiac which it replaced it was a dramatically different car – shorter yet with more interior space, and with greatly improved performance and handling. The Mark 2 car, introduced in 1977, was equally well received.

When the XJ6 Jaguar was introduced in 1968, it replaced three different models, which competed in three rather different segments of the market. Jaguar's new one-model policy certainly cleared up the former confusion, but it gave a headache to Chief Constables who had previously been happy to order the smallest Jaguar for their traffic fleets. As things turned out a number of forces went along with the XJ6, and were happy enough with the car. However it was undeniably on the large side, and it also managed to contract the unreliability disease from which all British-built models suffered during the late-seventies.

The fourth traffic car which might be said to typify the decade was the Range Rover. Although its performance, even with the same V8 engine as the 3500, was not outstanding, its vast carrying capacity could easily swallow all the equipment which traffic cars by now had to carry. And the issue of ultimate performance was increasingly under question, in an era where it was now the practice not to indulge in high-speed motorway chases but instead to trap a car at an exit. Performance apart, the Range Rover had all the qualities one could want, and many police forces ordered and re-ordered it.

So one could say that the seventies were both an end and a beginning. There was an end to a number of fine makes of car which had served police forces well in the past. And there was an end to a number of illusions about what was needed to compete in the modern world. Yet one could see a beginning, too, of trends that are still here today. Sex discrimination, for example, was outlawed in the seventies, which resulted in policewomen being given the same duties as their male colleagues. Amalgamations amongst police forces continued – and further ones are still being discussed today. As for the cars, those in use at that period still look more or less modern to our eyes now – but in another ten years or so they probably won't any more!

British Police Cars

Another example of the preference for vans for the more rural beat patrols. Once again a Morris 1000, with its useful extra height; it was in service with the Wiltshire force in 1970.

Below - Lancashire ordered the new Mk3 Ford Cortina for its traffic fleet in 1970. By now their traffic crews are wearing the new design of cap, with chequered band and white top.

Announced in 1968, the Jaguar XJ6's potential as a traffic car was clear to all; its combination of space, performance and road manners was unsurpassed. Staffordshire was one of many forces to use the model, as pictured here on the M6 motorway in 1971.

Below - Offering sports car performance with closed car comfort, the MGB GT was a popular choice for private buyers in the seventies. The Sussex force felt the same way, as demonstrated by the 1972 example shown here.

British Police Cars

By 1974 the Thames Valley traffic fleet had "gone foreign". The BMW 3.0S shown here was an ideal choice, combining space, carrying capacity and - importantly - reliability with superb performance. It is significant that the equivalent – and cheaper - Jaguar XJ6 was not judged to be acceptable.

By 1973 the Bedfordshire force had added Range Rovers to its fleet. Not only did they have the advantage of superior height, they also offered enormous carrying capacity. The display of equipment which could be packed inside this model is testimony to its load-lugging ability.

Right - Leicestershire was yet another force to be persuaded by the virtues of the Rover V8 3500. This 1975 model has the roof spotlights that were coming into use at that time. By now Leicestershire and Rutland had amalgamated with the Leicester City force and reverted to the simpler name of Leicestershire.

Yet another type of Ford in the Lancashire fleet, this time in 1975, was the Consul GT estate shown here. Effectively a Granada in size and engine capacity, it represented an attractive combination of space, performance and value-for-money.

British Police Cars

Left - The V8-engined Rover 3500 in police livery was one of the most common sights of the 1970s, both in London and elsewhere. Here a Metropolitan Police Rover escorts a wide load, probably around 1975. Note the roof spotlights, which were by this time a standard feature in most traffic fleets.

Right - The Mark 1 Granada, which Ford introduced in 1972 to replace the Mark 4 Zodiac, might have been designed with the police in mind. It was spacious inside, and its 3-litre engine gave the car remarkably good performance. Seen here is a 1977 model, which Leicestershire was using as an accident investigation car.

By the end of the seventies the Bedfordshire force was again using Fords as traffic cars. Here we see a Mark 2 Granada in 1979, in front of the then-new headquarters building in Kempston. The car is in what was then the recommended white livery with red stripe – known colloquially as the "jam sandwich".

These 1979 Mark 2 Granadas from the Warwickshire force have set up a road block somewhere in a rural part of the county. For once the photo appears to be of a real incident rather than one staged for the cameras. The actual date is probably some time in 1980.

British Police Cars

It was only in the mid-seventies that women police officers became entitled by law to carry out exactly the same duties as their male counterparts. Here a sergeant in the Bedfordshire force briefs a woman constable before the latter departs on a routine panda patrol.

Index

British Police Cars